Old CRAMOND

by

Peter and William J. S.

The Barnton Hotel is a landmark at the intersection of Whitehouse Road and Queensferry Road. Its name is a derivation of 'Barntoun' and can be dated to *c*.1400. On 1 March 1894 trains started running from Edinburgh to Barnton (previously the terminus had been Craigleith), and the hotel was built close to the station the following year, taking advantage of new, Victorian opportunities for travel. Barnton station served as one of two main access points from the city centre to the picturesque village of Cramond.

© Peter and William J. Scholes 2004
First published in the United Kingdom, 2004,
by Stenlake Publishing Ltd.
Telephone: 01290 551122
Printed by Cordfall Ltd., Glasgow G21 2QA

ISBN 1 84033 303 0

ACKNOWLEDGEMENTS

We would like to acknowledge with gratitude the willingness and courtesy of Cramond Heritage Trust in sharing its resources.

FURTHER READING

The books listed below were used by the authors during their research. None of them are available from Stenlake Publishing. Those interested in finding out more are advised to contact their local bookshop or reference library.

Cadell, P., *The Iron Mills at Cramond*, 1973
Cramond Heritage Trust, *Cramond Kirkyard Memorial Inscriptions*, 1993
Cramond Heritage Trust, *Cramond*, 1996
Dunlop, A. I., *The Kirks of Edinburgh 1560–1984*, 1985
Fraser, D., *Rhymes O' Auld Reekie*, 1973
Magnusson, M., *Scotland – The Story of a Nation*, 2000
McGlynn, M. Associates, *Historic Cramond Final Report*, prepared for City of Edinburgh Council, 2003
Rae, A. & V., *The Roman Fort at Cramond, Edinburgh, Excavations 1954–1966*, published in *Britannia* Vol. V, 1974
Smith, W. A. C. & Anderson, P., *Edinburgh's Railways*, 1995
The First and Second Statistical Accounts of the City of Edinburgh 1799 and 1845, 1998
The Third Statistical Account of Scotland, The City of Edinburgh, 1966
Wood, J., *The Antient and Modern State of the Parish of Cramond*, 1794, reprinted by Cramond Heritage Trust, 1994

Braepark Road leads from old Cramond Brig through Braehead.

INTRODUCTION

Cramond lies a few miles to the north-west of Edinburgh where the mouth of the River Almond forms a natural harbour as it joins the Firth of Forth. In 1790 its population of 299 families was found to be diminishing due to 'the removal of mechanics to town, the failure of the oyster fishing, and the increase of pasture ground' (*First Statistical Account*). Today it is a much sought-after residential suburb of the city, and its appeal attracts many tourists who enjoy its riverside walks and river crossing, its views of Fife, and the ambience of its dwellings that tell of a bygone age.

Cramond can legitimately claim to be a picture postcard village, for most of the images in this book have been reproduced from postcards and illustrate that from the beginning of the last century visitors came here to take the air, have a day out, or even enjoy a holiday. Indeed the royal seal of approval was given to Cramond in 1860. That year the Duchess of Kent, Queen Victoria's mother, had rented Cramond House and was in residence there. She was visited at Cramond by the Queen who attended a service at the kirk.

On entering Cramond's Glebe Road with its Victorian dwellings, one immediately has a sense of going back in time, and the village's historic past is now recognised as being of national importance. It is the site of the earliest recorded settlement in Scotland, dating from 8500–8200 BC. Excavation has revealed that units of the Roman army were garrisoned here, their presence dated by finds of pottery and coins from the early AD 140s left behind following the campaigns of emperors Antonius Pius and Septimius Severus. Structural evidence of administrative headquarters, granaries, workshops, latrines and a bathhouse remains, while the recent discovery of a Roman sculpture of a lioness, preserved over the centuries in the mud of the harbour, generated a worldwide wave of interest.

As surviving legacies of later ages Cramond has its early fifteenth century tower (originally associated with the bishops of Dunkeld), whilst its kirk, graveyard and laird's mansion combine to tell a tale of the times from the seventeenth century. The Old Schoolhouse is also part of that story and represents a period when the influence of the church on the community extended to education through a curriculum based on the three Rs, plus religious instruction for the many and Latin for the few. By way of complete contrast, upstream from the harbour a heritage of water-powered industry is revealed involving the smelting of Baltic pig iron into goods that were shipped all over the world.

The past is treasured and well-documented in Cramond. In an attempt to identify the best balance of conserving, managing and interpreting the village's archaeological remains and historic buildings, whilst giving access to one of Edinburgh's most beautiful areas, the city council has sought professional advice for that part of Cramond which lies within the area scheduled as an ancient monument. The careful implementation of that advice will ensure the well-being of the village's past and present for future generations.

The pictures in this book have been arranged into two overlapping sections, each of which provides a short walking (or armchair) tour, or may be combined into a pleasant and leisurely stroll. The numbers on the map refer to the pages the particular images appear on. The first section covers Cramond Glebe Road and Cramond village. From the junction of the former road and Whitehouse Road, near the bus stop, the route passes Cramond Kirk and the Roman fort and then continues down to the village, inn and harbour. From there the River Almond leads upstream to Cockle Mill and back to Whitehouse Road via School Brae.

The second section encompasses the River Almond and the iron mills. From Cockle Mill the Cramond Walkway provides access to Fairafar Mill, Peggy's Mill, Dowie's Mill and Cramond Brig, and thence through Braepark to Whitehouse Road and back to the village. The route can be shortened by leaving the walkway at Peggy's Mill. Diversions may be made to Barnton and along Gamekeeper's Road.

FAIRAFAR COTTAGES

This postcard is captioned 'The Glebe, Cramond'. The word 'glebe' means land which was attached to a parish church and which formed part of the minister's stipend. It was generally used for the growing of crops. Whilst the Victorian houses on the left (west) side of Cramond Glebe Road have remained largely unchanged over more than a century, the mode and pace of transport, as illustrated by the horse-drawn vehicle of Henry Baillie, contractor, have moved with the times.

Sent in 1904, this postcard shows the Manse of Cramond where the minister of Cramond Kirk and his family still stay. The central part of the house dates from 1649 when the entrance was situated on the south side. Extensions were added in the eighteenth and nineteenth centuries and the former stables for the minister's horse and carriage are to the rear. Excavation within the grounds of the manse in 1977–8 revealed part of the eastern defences of a Roman fort comprising ditches and a rampart.

796   CRAMOND PARISH CHURCH.

Cramond Kirk was rebuilt in 1656 on the site of a medieval building, which in its turn stood where the headquarters of a Roman fort had been located at a much earlier date. The kirk's ancient parish formerly stretched from the River Almond and the Firth of Forth to Granton, Blackhall, Clermiston and Cammo, and included Cramond Island. Now, due to the building of other churches in the area, the parish has been greatly reduced in size. The Dutch bell made by Michael Burgherhuys in 1619 was stolen from the fifteenth-century tower by Cromwell's Ironsides, but was subsequently returned after representation was made to General Monck by the Kirk Session. The church's list of post-Reformation ministers dates from 1575 and includes the Revd Robert Walker, who was the subject of Sir Henry Raeburn's portrait of the skating minister on Duddingston Loch, now to be seen in the National Gallery of Scotland. The earliest stone in the graveyard is that of John Stalker, 'an true and lively paterne of piety and probity', who died in 1608. His gravestone also notes that death comes to us all without exception, and around him lie iron-worker, collector of taxes, farm overseer, forester, inspector of the poor, minister, music seller, schoolmaster, stableman, weaver and wright. Both Cramond Kirk and its graveyard are Category A listed, denoting their historical significance.

Situated opposite the gates of the kirk, the Old Schoolhouse symbolises the vision of John Knox of a church and school in every parish. Built in 1778 at a cost of £148. 16s. 6d., it replaced a one-roomed building at the 'green-head of Nether Cramond' (thought to be the area near the old road behind and to the north of the graveyard), and served as both schoolhouse and home to the session clerks-cum-schoolmasters of Cramond Kirk until 1875, when the school moved to Almond Bank. The photograph shows John Smith, session clerk from 1871 to 1904, with friends and family in the grounds of the schoolhouse beneath a sycamore tree which still stands. One of his many responsibilities was the distribution of tea, coal and sugar to the poor of the parish. In 1794, when there were 70 to 80 scholars, John Wood noted that 'Cramond formerly was in great repute as a place of education, to which the salubrity of the air and vicinity of the sea did not a little contribute'. Between c.1643 and 2004 there were 21 session clerks of Cramond Kirk, of whom Ninian Paton's service of 52 years (1764–1816) is outstanding for its length. (Picture reproduced by courtesy of Dr W. E. S. Mutch.)

Cramond House.

Cramond House was built *c*.1680 by the Inglis family who previously lived in the adjacent Bishop's Tower. Its second proprietor, John Inglis, was a staunch Covenanter who was imprisoned for holding conventicles in the kirk. Cramond House was originally an integral part of the village and faced west on to the green, with the road down to the shore running between the house and the manse. Around 1778, in order to create an area of private parkland around the house, its owners had the kirkyard wall raised, the road closed and a new route opened through the minister's glebe (now Cramond Glebe Road). The church was compensated by the building of a parish school – out of view from the house. In 1860 Queen Victoria visited her mother, the Duchess of Kent, at Cramond House and described it as a 'really charming residence . . . quite near the sea with beautiful trees and very cheerful'. The chair used by Queen Victoria in Cramond Kirk still overlooks the pulpit.

CONVALESCENT SOLDIERS AT CRAMOND HOUSE, 1916.   R. BRAID.

Cramond House has had a chequered history. Once a prestigious mansion with extensive grounds, it served as a convalescent home for soldiers during the First World War (their names are listed in a register held in the Cramond archive) and in the 1960s enjoyed a brief spell as a nursing home. Having fallen into disrepair it was bought in 1971 by the Church of Scotland and subsequently restored in order to preserve the amenity of the area. It is currently leased to the Scottish Wildlife Trust. A ghostly female figure is said to have been seen in the house, which has also been claimed by some to be the original of R. L. Stevenson's 'House of Shaws'.

The stables for Cramond House were demolished in 1953 and the kirk hall built on the site. The walled gardens, summer house, potting sheds, glasshouses, kennels and ice house were also situated nearby. The eastern gate of the *Via Principalis* – the main street crossing the Roman fort – was in the vicinity of the stables and archaeological excavations here have brought to light important artefacts from Cramond's Roman occupation. Prior to excavation in the 1960s the presence of a Roman site had long been suspected because the area had yielded a variety of finds including coins, pottery and inscribed stones. (Picture reproduced by courtesy of Cramond Heritage Trust.)

A wintry view of Cramond showing a carriage outside the stables belonging to Henry Baillie where, apparently, cycles could also be stabled. In the late eighteenth century a domestic warren of 87 families comprising iron-workers, weavers, tailors, shoemakers, sailors, masons and labourers lived in the workers' houses of Nether Cramond. According to Wood (1794) their diet consisted of oatmeal for breakfast, sometimes with milk, potatoes prepared in a variety of ways and shellfish such as cockles and mussels. Flesh, fish and cheese were reported to be seldom tasted. Despite this basic fare and the 'intemperance of the lower classes', the health of those who lived in Nether Cramond was better than in other parts of the parish. Life though was short, infant mortality was high, and few villagers attained the age of 70. The local well lay in the woodland to the south of the Cramond Inn and in 1855 the village had its own post office (later transferred to Fairafar).

Cramond village *c*.1900 where some form of festive occasion involving young children and well-dressed adults is taking place at full tide. There seems to be an air of excitement and the event could have been a Sunday school outing. The partly obscured advertisement on the left is for Fry's Chocolate. An ancient festival called the Lammas Feast took place annually in the parish on 1 August and centred around the herd-boys who prevented cattle from straying on to farmers' crops. Having feasted on cream, butter and cheese on Corstorphine Hill to the east or Leny Hill to the west, members of the two parties marched to Cramond Muir behind a standard-bearer carrying an ensign made from a tablecloth, decorated with ribbons borrowed from girls of their acquaintance. En route a piper preceded the herd-boys who blew their horns. On meeting at Cramond Muir the weaker party was expected to lower its colours, but on occasion the issue was decided by force (particularly in 1734). Races were run before each party retired to its base to devote the evening to making merry.

A street busker entertains a group of touring cyclists (and dog) outside the crow-stepped Cramond Inn, which dates from 1670. The nearby Maltings, an earth-floored building with a wooden first floor for spreading out the grain to convert it into malt and domestic housing above that, was strategically sited in the complex opposite the inn. Three innkeepers lived in the village but there was only one inn.

Cramond Village

In 1792 the presence of seven licensed alehouses in the parish caused the Revd Bonar, the then minister of Cramond Kirk, to note the mournful corruption caused by these among the lower classes. He held that 'in few country parishes were the liberties and vices of the town any where more accurately copied'. The records of the Kirk Session do not remark on the potential conflict caused by the close proximity of the inn to Cramond Kirk. However, the session's members were vigilant in ensuring observation of the Sabbath, and punished those who engaged in 'tipling and tuilzieing' (drunk and disorderly conduct). Cramond Inn has featured in the Egon Ronay good food guide in recent years. This view shows the Victorian extension to the inn.

THE SHORE, CRAMOND 525.

Over the years Cramond's beach and shore have witnessed radical changes in function, beach attire, modes of entertainment and numbers of visitors. What has remained constant is the appeal and charm of the area. 'In the afternoon of a week-day in Cramond, there is a slumbrous peace . . . and almost the only sound is the slap of water against the boats'. (*Third Statistical Account*, 1966.)

Taken on river Almond, in the village of Cramond.

Rowing boats could be hired from Cramond's shore and further upstream at Cramond Brig. Originating 30 miles to the west, the waters of the Firth of Forth near the harbour were well suited for this seasonal pursuit, as was the River Almond.

The small windows, large number of chimneys and the washing on the lines combine to give an indication of the overcrowding, dampness and darkness that once prevailed in these houses. In the eighteenth century villagers lived six or more to a house with no running water and only primitive sanitation. Today Cramond Heritage Trust uses the Maltings to provide information to the public and mount displays about the area's past.

A canty neuk whaur Almond
    joins the Forth.
Ye dauner doun the brae
Wi' views o' Fife's green
    'Kingdom' to the north
Ayont the wee bit bay
Whaur Cramond Island rises
    frae the sand,
It's 'haufway' causey raxin oot
    frae land.

Amang the tombs the auld
    Kirk seems to hide
Wi' elms abune its heid.
The whitewashed biggins by
    the water side
Are crouned wi' tiles o' reid,
Whaur Charon, yachtin-
    capped (ye hae your
    penny?)
Will oar ye, no' to Hades, but
    Dalmeny.

The Kirk, the Inn, the Ferry –
    a' historic,
But lang afore their day
They spak a lingo here that
    wasna Doric:
Professor bodies say
That aince the Romans had a
    muckle fort
And diggin for its foonds is a'
    their sport.

From *Cramond*, by Douglas
    Fraser, 1973 (reproduced
    by permission of the poet's
    daughter, Mrs H. Moncur).

The picturesque workers' cottages and three-storied dwellings of Cramond village were not always as spick and span as they appear today. In 1958 Edinburgh Corporation served a closing order on 26 of the whitewashed two-apartment cottages, declaring them to be unfit for human habitation. At that time 54 Cramond people lived in what was described as a 'picturesque but tumbledown eighteenth century village'. Twenty years earlier restoration schemes for the villages of Cramond and Dean had been under consideration by the corporation, but were put into abeyance by the intervention of the war. The last of the original line of owners of Cramond House, Miss Dorothy Craigie-Halkett, offered to buy the condemned houses in 1959 and restore them at her own expense, but died before the purchase was complete. Her sole heir was not prepared to go ahead with his aunt's plans, but to its credit Edinburgh Corporation undertook the care of the village. On 3 July 1959 the Dean of Guild Court approved plans for restoration and modernisation at a cost of £27,040. Taken in August 1960, this photograph shows the work underway. (Picture reproduced by courtesy of *The Herald* & *Evening Times* Picture Archive.)

I. G. Lindsay and partners were the architects for the project and their plans were to convert the buildings into sixteen apartments of varying proportions, with the inclusion of one shop. The ground floors of some dwellings were to be let as stores. Though the interiors were to be radically altered, the buildings would retain their original appearance and be harled and lime-washed. Waste ground was to be grassed over or paved with granite setts, and eyesores such as the brick lavatories at the rear of the Glebe Road houses, and the manure dump between Glebe Road and the riverside were to become things of the past. (Picture reproduced by courtesy of Cramond Heritage Trust.)

The River Almond Cafe forlornly advertises its wares shortly before being swept away in the process of modernisation during which local families – some of whom had resided in the same house for four generations – were relocated to Davidson's Mains, Clermiston and other parts of the city. Nostalgia for the 'good old days' of Cramond should be tempered by recollections of the conditions in which the villagers were living in the latter half of the twentieth century. Despite the magnificent views, some tenants had to carry water in pails from a communal pump. The refurbished dwellings all had hot and cold running water, baths and proper sanitation. One who would note the changes was Charles Baillie, whose forebears drove the stagecoaches that plied to the city and the wagonettes that operated between Cramond and Barnton. (Picture reproduced by courtesy of Stewart Guthrie.)

THE SHORE, CRAMOND.

B.3967.

The shop shown in the right foreground of this 1950 view now styles itself as a bistro, while the harbour wall and esplanade that it faces were built up in the 1930s. Prior to then the surface of the causeway would have been of a primitive nature, muddy and scarred by cart tracks. Swans are now a feature on this stretch of water.

THE BEACH, CRAMOND.

B.8404.

The continuing increase in car ownership, greater amounts of available leisure time and the demands of modern-day recreation are issues with which Cramond is currently attempting to come to terms whilst retaining its identity. Now even its waters and beach have to comply with European standards. Dating from the 1950s, this view is indicative of the beginnings of these changes, and also harks back to a time when a day at the beach at Cramond could still draw a Costa del Sol sized crowd!

Highlighted here against the Fife coastline, Cramond Island is accessible to the public, tide permitting! Formerly the property of the bishops of Dunkeld, it served as an asylum for 'unfortunate females whose situation required a temporary retirement', according to the Kirk Session records of 1690, a practice of which the church strongly disapproved. Sins such as this usually invoked punishment for the transgressor on the stool of penitence (cutty stool). In 1690 a school of whales was stranded on the sands to the island's south side. A flock of Shetland and other sheep was put on it in the late eighteenth century in an experiment carried out by a group of pioneering agriculturalists including Lord Rosebery. The venture failed, but farming continued into the twentieth century when the parish's shoreline yielded about ten tons of kelp annually. During the Second World War an anti-shipping barrier was installed between the island and the mainland. Evidence of coastal batteries can still be seen.

THE FERRY, CRAMOND

Until 1662, when an Act of Parliament prevented access along the shore and past the house of Barnbougle in Dalmeny, a road ran 'betwixt the South Queens Ferrie and the Coble of Crawmond' and on to Edinburgh. The coble referred to was the Cramond ferry service across the River Almond. From September 1902 the backs of postcards were divided to allow messages as well as addresses, and the sender of a similar view to this one described the crossing in 1906 as 'just like a dream'. A century later the ferry is still sculled over the stern as it plies between Cramond Harbour and the ferryman's Coble Cottage on the west shore. Making the crossing and walking the few miles to Queensferry is a source of pleasure to many.

THE FERRY, CRAMOND

B.3966

In January 1997 the then ferryman, Robert Graham, began to investigate a detached piece of rock which he had noticed protruding through the mud at the foot of the Cramond steps at low tide. The rock appeared to have been carved and archaeologists were alerted. Journalists and TV cameras were soon on site to announce unfolding events to the world as the strange rock was unearthed *in situ* and then lifted above the harbour wall.

Soon news flashed around the world that the 1.5 metre long, 75 cm high carved rock dated from Roman times and represented a crouching lioness whose paws rested on a man's shoulders with his head in its mouth. Parts of the base had broken off but were found and later reattached. The pale sandstone from which the lioness was carved was not of local origin (but may have come from Alloa), and the sculpture is thought to date from the second or early third century AD during the occupation of the Roman fort at Cramond. It is possible that it had a funerary significance and symbolised the power of death, with the snakes on the base representing the survival of the soul. The depiction of carnivores such as lions (intended to ward off the evil eye) devouring prey appears commonly in the symbolism of Roman funerary sculptures, although the combination of subjects represented in the Cramond lioness is unique. Numerous questions remain unanswered about the remarkable discovery. These include whether it was originally one of a pair of sculptures, and whether it formed part of a memorial to an important Roman dignitary stationed at the fort. Under Scots law the find was declared to be treasure trove and the ferryman rewarded. His five-figure payment was decided by Scotland's Crown Agent after consultation with a panel of experts on the value of the statue. The lioness is now in the joint care of the City of Edinburgh Council and the National Museums of Scotland, but it is hoped that it will be returned to Cramond for permanent display in due course. (Picture reproduced by courtesy of Valerie E. Dean.)

Another of the unsolved mysteries surrounding the lioness is how it came to be embedded in the estuarial mud of the river. The level of the Almond is lower at Cramond than it was in Roman times, and whenever the sculpture sank to its resting place the water was deeper than it is today. Could it have been lost overboard during loading or unloading operations in the harbour? Part of this debate includes conjecture that it may have been deliberately dumped. Whatever the answers to these and other questions, archaeologically the discovery of the lioness highlighted the significance of the Roman fort at Cramond. (Picture reproduced by courtesy of Judy C. Dean.)

Eagle Rock, situated along the Dalmeny shoreline, is said to bear a representation of an eagle carved during Cramond's period of Roman occupation. Cramond was one of three coastal forts which were built along the shores of the Firth of Forth (Carriden lies to the west and Inveresk to the east). These served as strategic strongholds beyond the eastern end of the Antonine Wall, which stretched between the Clyde and Forth estuaries, and helped protect the Roman-occupied territory of southern Scotland.

Viewed from the air or the grounds of Dalmeny estate (which belongs to the Earl of Rosebery), a wider perspective is gained of Cramond's tidal estuary. The west gallery of the kirk is still referred to as the Dalmeny gallery, reflecting a time when Sunday attendance was virtually obligatory and rights to seated portions of a church could be purchased by wealthy individuals such as local lairds. The remainder of the congregation sat on stools brought in by themselves, or leaned against the walls during the service which lasted three hours. This photograph was taken prior to the construction of the promenade, and thus in the absence of steps those who wished to use the ferry would have had to walk across a plank to board it. Following the river upstream, the site of an early boat club can be seen, as well as a corner of the bowling green whose championship trophy was last awarded in 1932.

The River Almond Cafe was in business when this 1952 postcard view of the foreshore was produced, and presents a tidier appearance than in the picture on page 18, prior to its demolition as part of the restoration and modernisation of the dwellings in the village. The steps between the cafe and the building containing the shop lead up to Cramond Glebe Road and the Cramond Inn. Cars no longer have public access to the foreshore.

Several hundred metres upstream along the Cramond Walkway the former offices of Cockle Mill come into view. The River Almond was once navigable to this point at high tide, and the dock for unloading and loading the 40- to 50-ton vessels that berthed here remains. Originally the site of a grain mill dating from the twelfth century and known as Cramond Mill, the riverbank was occupied by ironworks used to manufacture products from raw materials shipped in from Russia, Sweden and Holland from 1750 onwards. Bar iron was heated, rolled and made into barrel hoops, pot handles, pans for saltworks, and most commonly the square-section nails characteristic of the eighteenth century. In 1759 the Carron Company of Falkirk took over Cockle Mill, and one of its founders, William Cadell, is remembered in the name of Caddell's (*sic*) Row, which was given to the buildings overlooking the river which were used to house the iron-workers. The Cadells' lengthy association with iron-working at Cramond is also recalled in the kirkyard, where several of their graves lie, while the nails used to build the Old Schoolhouse were supplied by the same family. Cockle Mill is said to take its name from the cockle weed which grew among the corn crops.

Cockle Mill was the first of four mills between Cramond and Cramond Brig on the east side of the river, all of which were owned at one time by the company of Cadell & Edington. Thomas Edington went on to establish a reputation as one of the great ironmasters of the West of Scotland. In the mid-nineteenth century Cockle Mill's forge, slitting and rolling mills gave employment to about twenty men. The presence of an industrial undertaking in a parish in which there were fourteen large farms (and twelve smaller ones) supplying the needs of Edinburgh altered the means of livelihood for a number of parishioners, and also led to legal disputes. Lord Rosebery objected to the presence of sailors and 'other disorderly persons' using the west bank of the river between Cockle Mill and the harbour as a towpath for hauling boats. He also held that salmon fishing on the Almond had been impaired by the erection of dams. In 1867 the schoolmaster John Milne complained to the heritors that the plaster of Cramond's schoolhouse was cracking due to vibrations from the large mill hammers.

Cockle Mill's development under the ironmasters began in 1752 when a consortium of local merchants and shipowners feued it from Sir John Inglis of Cramond House and began the manufacture of small forgings and agricultural implements. From 1759 the mill became associated with the newly-formed Carron Company at Falkirk, but when the large blast furnaces there went into full operation, Cockle Mill's slit mill became irrelevant, and in 1770 Cadell and Edington took it over themselves. The pattern established at Cockle Mill of workers' cottages being built near to the mill on the rising ground of the valley was adopted for the subsequent industrial developments upstream.

A horse tramway for transporting coal and iron to the ironworks – and finished products from them – ran between Fairafar and Cockle Mills and up School Brae. The salmon ladder is still present on the west side of Fairafar Mill's impressive waterfall, but the supply of fish diminished from the eighteenth century onwards because of the liming of the adjacent land. Originally a grain mill, then a wauk mill, Fairafar's waterwheel latterly powered a tilt hammer which was used to make files, girdles and agricultural implements. Water power was replaced by steam shortly after the mid-point of the nineteenth century.

The Old Mills & Waterfall, Cramond.

ROAD TO PEGGY'S MILL, CRAMOND

R & W. E.

Despite being the last of the four mills between Cramond and Cramond Brig to remain in operation, little trace of Peggy's Mill can now be found. As the demand for ironwork lessened after the Napoleonic Wars, Peggy's Mill tried to diversify into the production of paper. However, by 1881 the water of the River Almond had proved to be unsuitable for this purpose and the mill converted to the manufacture of gelatine until 1922, finishing its days in the mid-1930s with furniture-making. Even this postcard of 1908 showing Peggy's Mill Road gives a rather desolate impression. Situated on the opposite bank of the river between Peggy's Mill and Fairafar Mill, Craigie Mill was the only mill on the Dalmeny estate. It seems to have been less commercially successful than those on the Cramond side and by 1740 was in a state of decay.

This postcard showing Dowie's Mill from Cramond Brig bears a ha'penny stamp from the reign of King Edward VII and was franked in 1903. In 1841 the colony of workers' houses accommodated a population of 77, of whom 28 were employed at the mills. A charter of 1697 referred to Dowie's as the 'old' mill and Peggy's as the 'new' mill.

Like the other Cramond mills, Dowie's was originally a grain mill. Under Cadell and Edington's ownership from 1782, it principally manufactured spades before turning to saw-milling and furniture-making in the twentieth century. The weir had a fall of more than 2.3 metres and supplied water to the mill through two sluice gates. Despite having been breached, the 'damheid' (weir) at Dowie's Mill is well-preserved. Primrose Cottage, facing the mill, may either reflect the family name of the owners of Dalmeny estate, or the flower of the same name.

THE AULD BRIG. CRAMOND.

Cramond Brig marked the boundary between Edinburghshire and Linlithgowshire and carried the turnpike road over the River Almond. The date on the central arch is 1619, although an Act of Parliament of 1587 noted that the bridge had been ruinous for a long time and thus it must have served as a crossing point from much earlier in the sixteenth century. In 1823 a new eight-arch bridge was constructed upstream by John Rennie, an engineer from London, to accommodate the increase in traffic. As a young man Rennie had reported on the mill machinery at Cockle Mill in 1782. Construction of his bridge meant that access across the River Almond on the turnpike road was made easier, allowing the Aberdeen coach to travel the ten mile stage from Queensferry to Edinburgh in 50 minutes without a change of horses. On his death Rennie's two sons continued the link between his family and civil engineering.

The pool of water adjacent to the Auld Brig was created by the dam at Dowie's Mill, and was once used for recreational boating. The footpath on the Cramond side leads to Braepark whilst the Cramond Brig Hotel can be glimpsed in the background on the opposite side of the river.

OLD CRAMOND BRIG

The 1619 Cramond Brig was closed to vehicular traffic in 1986 and is now an A-listed structure. Judging by the rural scenes depicted on this postcard and the one on the facing page, both dating from the turn of the twentieth century, the new turnpike bridge of 1823 had so diminished the flow of traffic that the old bridge was serving as a haven for the neighbouring community by this date.

This view entitled 'At Auld Cramond Brig' is typical of many Edwardian postcards, in that individuals have been posed to give depth to the scene. Here the blooms of the fruiterer are displayed to good effect, but the lad in the foreground has bare feet. Both this picture and the previous one were taken from the west side of the bridge. The lower lintel of the old tollhouse bears the date 1648.

Jock Howison's cottage stood on the east bank of the river, upstream from Cramond Brig. According to local tradition Jock was a peasant who, armed with a flail, came to the rescue of a stranger being attacked in the vicinity of the bridge. Later he learned that the horseman whom he had rescued was King James V (1513–42) who in gratitude granted him the lands of Braehead, in return for which he and his successors were to provide the monarch with a basin of water and napkin to wash their hands if requested. When George IV visited Edinburgh in 1822 Sir Walter Scott re-enacted the ceremony at a banquet at Holyrood, and a similar re-enactment took place in 1937 with George V. In 1966, when Queen Elizabeth II was en route to the opening of the new Tay Bridge, she acknowledged the offering near the site of Jock Howison's cottage. Credence to the legend, which is the subject of a glass mosaic panel in Cramond Kirk, is given by the royal ceremonial role of 'Washer of the Sovereign's Hands' still held by Jock Howison's descendants. However, whilst a handsome statue south-east of the new bridge at Braehead Mains records that James V was attacked at Cramond Brig in 1532, an alternative view attributes the tale to Sir Walter Scott, who wrote of the Guidman (tenant) of Ballengeich, a name used by James V when travelling in disguise, in his *Tales of a Grandfather*.

Cramond Brig Hotel is sited to the north of the river crossing from which it takes its name, with the road to the old bridge running immediately behind it. An inn on this site is recorded on a map dated 1853. In keeping with the march of progress, Rennie's bridge was blown up in 1963 using 530 lbs of gelignite distributed over 1,700 phased charges to make way for the present structure – a delicate operation since the two were only feet apart.

When Cramond toll was moved to the new bridge in 1823, the following scale of charges was established:

Stage coach with no more than six passengers inside and none outside: 2s, 6d
Two or more outside passengers: 3s, 6d
Other single horse or beast of draught drawn barouche or chariot: 1s, 3d
Saddled horse, mare or gelding, laden or unladen mule: 3d
Laden or unladen ass: 2d

As commuters from Fife to Edinburgh will readily attest, and despite speed restrictions, the current Cramond Bridge is seldom as peaceful as this scene from the 1920s suggests it was then.

RIVER ALMOND AND BRAEPARK, CRAMOND BRIG.   937.

According to John Wood's book *The Antient and Modern State of the Parish of Cramond* (1794), the Howison family of Braehead was the longest-established in the parish, 'having subsisted in this district upwards of 330 years'. Braepark Road leads from Dowie's Mill and the old bridge through Braehead, the former estate of the Howisons.

Long Row (right), cuts in from the higher ground as Braepark Road leads up from the river valley. The photographer on this occasion was John McKean, who c.1895 took a number of photographs of Cramond, many of which were later used as commercial postcards and appear as such in this book. McKean gave character and atmosphere to his compositions by careful use of local residents to enhance his pictures. As well as Cramond and the River Almond his subjects included Leith, Bonnington, Newhaven and Barnton. He was listed in the 1881 census as being aged 31 and with two children. Other nineteenth century photographers of Cramond included J. C. H. Balmain and J. R. Russell. (Picture reproduced by courtesy of Cramond Heritage Trust.)

The gates of Barnton House stand opposite Braepark Road where it meets Whitehouse Road. The house (formerly called Cramond Regis) dated from *c.*1640 and was built by Sir John Smith of Grotthill who had been a provost of Edinburgh. The parkland in which Barnton House stood – now occupied by the Royal Burgess Golfing Society and the Bruntsfield Links Golfing Society – once served as a royal hunting estate. When the house was demolished in 1925 the gates remained at the crossroads, and were later resited when the road was widened in the 1970s.

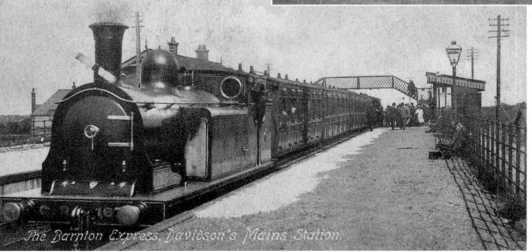

The Barnton Express Davidson's Mains Station.

The single-track suburban service from Princes Street station was extended from Craigleith to Barnton for passenger and goods traffic in 1894. Local schoolchildren were given a half-day holiday to celebrate the event. Here the Barnton Express is seen at Davidson's Mains station, the stop preceding Barnton, shortly after the line opened.

Barnton Station, Cramond Bridge.

This view shows individuals leaving the railway station at Barnton on foot, whilst carriages are on hand for other travellers. The stop at Davidson's Mains was originally called Barnton Gate, and the station at Barnton was called Cramond Brig, but in 1903 they were renamed Davidson's Mains and Barnton respectively. In the Edwardian era there were 24 trains daily between Princes Street and Barnton, with an extra five being run on Saturdays. In summer there was even a Sunday service to cater for day-trippers to Cramond. By 1930 the service had begun to be cut back due to increases in car ownership.

The fleet of vehicles shown here is that of Henry Baillie of Cramond, who took advantage of the opening of the railway station by providing carriages to Cramond, in addition to a carriage and carting service from the village to Edinburgh. Introduced in the mid-1890s, Baillie's horse-drawn service remained operational for more than 60 years, despite technological advances. The station at Barnton was a powerful influence in persuading the Royal Burgess Golfing Society to relocate from Musselburgh to the Maitland estate at Barnton, and in 1895 its new golf course – designed by Tom Morris – was opened, with the clubhouse (background) following two years later. When Barnton station closed in 1951, the bell which had alerted the golfers to the imminent departure of trains back to Edinburgh was purchased by the RBGS.

CARGILFIELD SCHOOL. (J.P.)

Gamekeeper's Road branches off Whitehouse Road midway between Barnton and Cramond, opposite Peggy's Mill Road. Here Scotland's first preparatory school may be seen. Founded in 1873 by the Revd Charles Darnell, Cargilfield moved to its present location from Trinity in Edinburgh in 1896 when the terms for boarders were 80 guineas for the under-tens and 90 guineas for older pupils. The fees for day boys were 20 guineas. Cargilfield is situated between courses belonging to two of the oldest golf clubs in the world, the Royal Burgess Golfing Society (1735) and Bruntsfield Links Golfing Society (1761). The histories of the two clubs show a remarkable correlation. Both initially played on the Bruntsfield, a piece of land forming part of the city's Burgh Muir; both moved to Musselburgh, establishing separate clubhouses but sharing their links with the Honourable Company of Edinburgh Golfers (1744) and the Royal Musselburgh Golf Club (1774); and both moved to their present, adjoining locations in the 1890s.

FAIR - A - FAR,
CRAMOND.

Fairafar Cottages took their name from the mill of the same name on the River Almond and initially provided homes for the families of local iron-workers. The economical nature of their design is similar to that adopted for workers' cottages in other parts of the city with stairs to the rear. At the turn of the twentieth century there was a post office, a general merchant's store and Mrs Rankin's 'refreshment rooms' in the vicinity of the cottages.

Almond Bank and the Glebe. Cramond

The two-storey Almond Bank Cottages predominantly housed employees from Cramond's ironworks. On one side they are flanked by a large stone house, built in 1778 for one of the partners of the company which owned the riverside mills. The cottages on the other side leading to The Glebe were converted to form a primary school in 1875 to meet the demands of the 1872 Education (Scotland) Act. They now serve as a private nursery. John Smith was the schoolmaster and session clerk at the time of the removal of the former church-governed school from Cramond Glebe Road to Almond Bank, and was the last of Cramond's long line of similar appointees. He is buried in the kirk graveyard.

ALMOND BANK AND GLEBE, CRAMOND.

Built in the 1890s, these desirable houses on The Glebe look over to Cramond Green and appear similar today as they did a century ago. They mark the conclusion of this tour of old Cramond. Over several centuries the village has undergone a change from a pastoral landscape to one of heavy industry, with desirable housing now its dominant feature. As this group of male figures walks towards the former glebe, perhaps wearing their Sunday best, they leave Almond Bank Cottages and the former village school behind them.